CHRIS DEVON

Python Serverless Framework For Beginners

Contents

Introduction

What is Serverless Architecture?

Serverless architecture is a cloud computing model that enables developers to build and run applications without having to manage the underlying infrastructure. This approach allows developers to focus on writing code and developing features while the cloud provider takes care of the server management, scaling, and resource allocation. Here's a comprehensive overview of serverless architecture, its components, benefits, and potential use cases.

Definition and Key Concepts

At its core, serverless architecture allows developers to deploy code in the cloud without the need to provision or manage servers. The term "serverless" can be misleading; it does not mean that servers are completely absent. Instead, it refers to the abstraction of server management responsibilities, allowing developers to operate at a higher level of abstraction.

Key concepts in serverless architecture include:

- **Functions as a Service (FaaS)**: The primary component of serverless architecture. FaaS allows developers to write single-purpose functions that are executed in response to events. Each function runs in a stateless compute container and scales automatically based on demand.
- **Event-Driven Execution**: Serverless applications are often built around

events that trigger function execution. Events can originate from various sources, such as HTTP requests, changes to databases, file uploads, or message queues.

- **Managed Services**: In addition to FaaS, serverless architecture often incorporates other managed services such as databases (e.g., AWS DynamoDB), storage solutions (e.g., AWS S3), and messaging services (e.g., AWS SNS or SQS). These services simplify application development by providing ready-to-use components that integrate seamlessly.

How Serverless Architecture Works

1. **Code Deployment**: Developers write code in the form of functions, typically in languages like Python, Node.js, or Java. This code is deployed to a serverless platform, where it is packaged and made available for execution.

2. **Event Triggering**: Functions are triggered by events. For example, a function might execute when a user uploads a file to a cloud storage bucket or when an API endpoint is called.

3. **Execution and Scaling**: When an event occurs, the cloud provider automatically provisions the necessary resources to execute the function. The function runs in a stateless environment, meaning it does not retain data between executions. If multiple events occur simultaneously, the cloud provider can scale the execution by launching additional instances of the function.

4. **Billing**: One of the key advantages of serverless architecture is the pay-as-you-go pricing model. Developers only pay for the compute time consumed during the execution of their functions, rather than for idle server time. This can lead to significant cost savings, especially for applications with variable or unpredictable workloads.

Benefits of Serverless Architecture

1. **Reduced Operational Overhead**: Serverless architecture eliminates

the need for developers to manage server provisioning, scaling, and maintenance, allowing them to focus on writing code and delivering features.

2. **Scalability**: Serverless applications can automatically scale based on demand. This is particularly beneficial for applications with fluctuating workloads, as the cloud provider handles scaling without intervention.

3. **Cost Efficiency**: The pay-as-you-go model allows businesses to only pay for the resources they use, making it a cost-effective option for startups and organizations with varying workloads.

4. **Faster Time to Market**: By abstracting infrastructure management, serverless architecture enables faster development cycles, allowing teams to iterate and deploy applications more quickly.

5. **Enhanced Reliability**: Serverless platforms often come with built-in redundancy and high availability, ensuring that applications remain operational even in the face of failures.

Use Cases for Serverless Architecture

1. **Web Applications**: Serverless architecture is well-suited for building modern web applications that require high availability and scalability.

2. **APIs and Microservices**: Developing RESTful APIs and microservices can benefit from the event-driven model of serverless, allowing for independent deployment and scaling of services.

3. **Data Processing**: Serverless functions can process data streams, run batch jobs, or handle event-driven workflows, making it ideal for data-intensive applications.

4. **IoT Applications**: The scalability and event-driven nature of serverless architecture make it an excellent choice for Internet of Things (IoT) applications, which often generate numerous events that need processing.

5. **Automation and Scheduled Tasks**: Serverless functions can automate routine tasks, such as database backups, report generation, or image processing, based on specific triggers or schedules.

Serverless architecture represents a paradigm shift in how applications are developed and deployed. By removing the complexity of server management, it empowers developers to build scalable, cost-effective, and efficient applications that can respond to real-time events. As organizations increasingly seek agility and efficiency in their development processes, serverless architecture is likely to play a crucial role in the future of cloud computing and application development.

Why Choose Python for Serverless Applications?

Python has gained significant popularity as a programming language, particularly in the realm of serverless architecture. Its simplicity, versatility, and strong community support make it an excellent choice for building serverless applications. Here are several reasons why Python stands out in this context:

1. **Ease of Learning and Use**

Python's straightforward syntax and readability make it an ideal language for beginners and experienced developers alike. This ease of use allows developers to quickly write, test, and deploy serverless functions without getting bogged down in complex syntax or verbose code. The simplicity of Python also enables teams to onboard new developers more rapidly, facilitating collaboration and enhancing productivity.

2. **Rich Ecosystem and Libraries**

Python boasts a vast ecosystem of libraries and frameworks that can significantly accelerate development. Whether it's data manipulation (using libraries like Pandas and NumPy), web development (Flask and Django), or machine learning (TensorFlow and Scikit-learn), Python has a tool for almost any task. This rich library ecosystem allows developers to leverage existing solutions, reducing the need to build everything from scratch and enabling them to focus on core application logic.

3. Strong Community Support

Python has a large and active community that contributes to its continuous improvement. This community provides a wealth of resources, including tutorials, forums, and documentation, making it easier for developers to find solutions to their challenges. Community support is particularly beneficial in serverless architecture, where developers can share best practices, troubleshooting tips, and innovative approaches to common problems.

4. Integration with Major Cloud Providers

Most major cloud platforms, such as AWS, Google Cloud, and Azure, offer robust support for Python in their serverless offerings. For instance, AWS Lambda allows developers to write functions in Python and provides seamless integration with other AWS services like DynamoDB, S3, and API Gateway. This compatibility with cloud services simplifies the development and deployment process, enabling developers to build comprehensive applications quickly.

5. Versatility Across Domains

Python is a versatile language that excels in various domains, including web development, data science, automation, and artificial intelligence. This versatility allows developers to use the same language across different components of an application. For example, a serverless function written in Python can easily interface with a data analysis library to process incoming data from an IoT device or perform machine learning predictions on demand.

6. Asynchronous Programming Support

Python supports asynchronous programming through libraries such as asyncio, which is particularly beneficial in serverless applications that often involve I/O-bound operations, such as database queries or API calls. By leveraging asynchronous programming, developers can optimize the performance of their serverless functions, ensuring they run efficiently and reduce latency.

7. Rapid Development and Prototyping

The combination of Python's simplicity, rich libraries, and strong community support facilitates rapid application development. Developers can quickly prototype ideas and iterate on them, which is crucial in fast-paced development environments. This rapid iteration capability is particularly advantageous for startups and organizations looking to bring their products to market swiftly.

8. Strong Support for Data Processing and Analytics

Python's prominence in data processing and analytics makes it a preferred choice for serverless applications that involve data manipulation. With powerful libraries for data analysis, such as Pandas and NumPy, developers can efficiently process and analyze data streams, making Python a go-to option for data-intensive serverless functions.

Choosing Python for serverless applications brings numerous advantages, including ease of use, a rich ecosystem, strong community support, and compatibility with major cloud providers. Its versatility across various domains and robust capabilities for asynchronous programming and data processing further enhance its appeal. As organizations increasingly adopt serverless architecture, Python's role as a leading language in this space is likely to grow, making it a compelling choice for developers looking to leverage the benefits of serverless computing.

Getting Started with Python

Setting Up Your Python Environment

Before diving into serverless development with Python, it's essential to set up your Python environment correctly. This chapter will guide you through the process of installing Python and selecting the right Integrated Development Environment (IDE) and tools to optimize your development experience.

Installing Python

1. Downloading Python

The first step in setting up your Python environment is to download the latest version of Python. Python is available for various operating systems, including Windows, macOS, and Linux.

- **Visit the Official Python Website**: Go to python.org to access the official Python downloads page.
- **Choose the Right Version**: Select the latest stable version of Python. As of now, Python 3.x is the recommended version, as Python 2 has reached the end of its life.

2. Installation Process

- **For Windows:**

- Download the Python installer (a .exe file).
- Run the installer. Make sure to check the box that says "Add Python to PATH" during the installation process. This option allows you to run Python commands from the command prompt.
- Follow the installation prompts to complete the setup.
- **For macOS:**
- Download the Python installer (a .pkg file) from the Python website.
- Run the installer and follow the instructions.
- Alternatively, you can use the Homebrew package manager by running the command brew install python in the Terminal.
- **For Linux:**
- Most Linux distributions come with Python pre-installed. You can check by running python3 —version in the terminal.
- If Python is not installed, you can install it using the package manager. For Ubuntu and Debian-based systems, use the command:

```
sudo apt update
sudo apt install python3
```

- For Red Hat-based systems, use:

```
sudo yum install python3
```

3. Verifying the Installation

After installation, it's important to verify that Python is correctly installed:

- Open a command prompt (Windows) or terminal (macOS/Linux).

- Type the following command and press Enter:

```
python --version
```

- or, in some systems, you might need to use:

```
python3 --version
```

- You should see the version of Python displayed, confirming that the installation was successful.

IDE and Tool Selection

Choosing the right IDE and tools can significantly enhance your productivity as you develop serverless applications with Python. Here are some popular options to consider:

1. Integrated Development Environments (IDEs)

- **Visual Studio Code (VS Code):**
- A lightweight and powerful code editor developed by Microsoft, VS Code supports Python development through extensions.
- Features include IntelliSense (code completion), debugging tools, integrated terminal, and extensive marketplace for additional functionalities.
- To set up Python in VS Code:
- Install the Python extension from the marketplace.
- Configure the Python interpreter to point to your Python installation.
- **PyCharm:**
- Developed by JetBrains, PyCharm is a full-featured IDE specifically

designed for Python development.
- It includes features like code navigation, refactoring, and support for web frameworks, making it suitable for serverless applications.
- The Community edition is free, while the Professional edition offers additional features for web and data science development.
- **Jupyter Notebook**:
- Ideal for data science and machine learning projects, Jupyter Notebook allows you to create interactive notebooks that combine code, visualizations, and narrative text.
- It's particularly useful for prototyping and experimenting with serverless functions that involve data manipulation.
- **Thonny**:
- A beginner-friendly IDE that comes with Python bundled, Thonny is an excellent choice for those just starting with Python.
- It features a simple interface, debugging capabilities, and a built-in Python shell, making it easy to learn and use.

2. Command-Line Interface (CLI) Tools

- **pip**:
- pip is the package installer for Python, allowing you to install and manage additional libraries and dependencies. It comes pre-installed with Python.
- To install a package, use the command:

```
pip install package_name
```

- **virtualenv**:
- Virtual environments allow you to create isolated environments for your Python projects, ensuring that dependencies do not conflict between

projects.
- To install virtualenv, run:

```
pip install virtualenv
```

- To create a virtual environment:

```
virtualenv myenv
```

- Activate it (Windows):

```
myenv\Scripts\activate
```

- Activate it (macOS/Linux):

```
source myenv/bin/activate
```

- **Docker**:
- While not exclusively for Python, Docker allows you to containerize your applications, providing a consistent development environment that can be easily deployed in serverless environments.

- Learning Docker basics can be beneficial as you scale your serverless applications.

Setting up your Python environment is the foundational step in embarking on your journey into serverless application development. By installing Python and choosing the right IDE and tools, you equip yourself with the necessary resources to write efficient, scalable, and maintainable code. With your environment ready, you are now prepared to explore the exciting world of Python serverless frameworks and the possibilities they offer.

Basic Python Concepts

Before diving deeper into serverless application development, it's essential to understand some basic Python concepts. This section will cover fundamental data types and structures, as well as functions and error handling in Python.

Data Types and Structures

Python is a dynamically typed language, meaning you don't need to explicitly declare the data type of a variable when you create it. Python provides several built-in data types, which can be categorized into various structures. Here are the key data types and structures you will encounter:

1. Basic Data Types

- **Integers (int)**: Whole numbers, both positive and negative.

```python
python
```

```
age = 30
```

- **Floating Point Numbers (float)**: Numbers with a decimal point.

```python
price = 19.99
```

- **Strings (str)**: A sequence of characters enclosed in single or double quotes.

```python
name = "John Doe"
```

- **Booleans (bool)**: Represents True or False values.

```python
is_active = True
```

2. Data Structures

Python provides several built-in data structures that allow you to store collections of data. The most commonly used ones include:

- **Lists**: An ordered collection of items that can be of different data types. Lists are mutable, meaning you can change their content.

```python

fruits = ["apple", "banana", "cherry"]
```

- **Tuples**: Similar to lists, but immutable, meaning their content cannot be changed after creation. Tuples are defined using parentheses.

```python

coordinates = (10.0, 20.0)
```

- **Dictionaries (dict)**: A collection of key-value pairs, where each key is unique. Dictionaries are unordered and mutable.

```python

user = {"name": "Alice", "age": 25}
```

- **Sets**: An unordered collection of unique items. Sets are useful for operations that require uniqueness and membership testing.

```python

unique_numbers = {1, 2, 3, 4, 5}
```

3. Type Conversion

Python allows for implicit and explicit type conversion. Implicit conversion occurs automatically, while explicit conversion requires using functions like int(), float(), and str() to convert between types.

```python
number_str = "100"
number_int = int(number_str)  # Converts string to integer
```

Functions and Error Handling

Functions are a fundamental building block in Python, allowing you to encapsulate code for reuse and organization. Error handling is crucial for creating robust applications by managing exceptions that may arise during execution.

1. Defining Functions

Functions in Python are defined using the def keyword, followed by the function name and parentheses. You can pass parameters to functions and return values.

```python
def greet(name):
    return f"Hello, {name}!"

message = greet("Alice")
print(message)  # Output: Hello, Alice!
```

2. Function Parameters

- **Positional Parameters**: Arguments are passed based on their position.
- **Keyword Parameters**: You can specify arguments by name, allowing for more clarity.

```python
python

def add(a, b):
    return a + b

result = add(b=5, a=3)  # Keyword arguments
```

- **Default Parameters**: You can provide default values for parameters, which will be used if no value is provided.

```python
python

def multiply(a, b=2):
    return a * b

print(multiply(5))  # Output: 10
```

3. Returning Values

Functions can return a single value or multiple values in the form of a tuple.

```python
python

def calculate(x, y):
    return x + y, x * y

sum_result, product_result = calculate(3, 4)
```

4. Error Handling with Exceptions

Error handling in Python is done using try and except blocks. This allows you to manage errors gracefully without crashing the program.

```python
python
```

```
try:
    result = 10 / 0  # This will raise a ZeroDivisionError
except ZeroDivisionError:
    print("Cannot divide by zero.")
finally:
    print("Execution completed.")
```

- **Multiple Exceptions**: You can handle multiple types of exceptions in a single except block.

python

```
try:
    number = int(input("Enter a number: "))
except ValueError:
    print("That's not a valid number!")
```

- **Custom Exceptions**: You can define your own exceptions by subclassing the built-in Exception class.

python

```
class MyCustomError(Exception):
    pass

try:
    raise MyCustomError("An error occurred!")
except MyCustomError as e:
    print(e)
```

Understanding basic Python concepts, including data types, structures, functions, and error handling, is essential for building effective serverless applications. These foundational elements provide the tools you need to write efficient, organized, and robust code. As you progress through this book, these concepts will serve as the building blocks for your serverless projects, enabling you to tackle more complex challenges with confidence.

Understanding Serverless Frameworks

Overview of Serverless Frameworks

Serverless frameworks are powerful tools that simplify the development and deployment of serverless applications. They provide developers with a set of abstractions and utilities to manage infrastructure, code, and services without having to worry about the underlying server management. This chapter will explore what serverless frameworks are, their benefits, and the most popular options available today.

What is a Serverless Framework?

A serverless framework is a development framework that allows developers to build and deploy applications in a serverless architecture. These frameworks provide an environment for defining functions, configuring resources, managing deployments, and integrating with other cloud services.

Key characteristics of serverless frameworks include:

- **Abstraction of Infrastructure**: Developers can focus on writing business logic while the framework handles the provisioning and scaling of resources in the cloud.
- **Event-Driven Architecture**: Serverless frameworks support event-driven programming, allowing developers to define functions that automatically execute in response to specific events.
- **Configuration as Code**: Most frameworks use configuration files (often

in YAML or JSON format) to define services, resources, and functions, making it easy to version control and manage infrastructure.

Benefits of Using Serverless Frameworks

1. **Rapid Development**: Serverless frameworks streamline the development process by providing templates and built-in integrations, enabling developers to build and deploy applications quickly.
2. **Cost Efficiency**: By utilizing a serverless framework, developers only pay for the compute time their functions use, making it a cost-effective option, especially for applications with variable workloads.
3. **Simplified Scaling**: Serverless frameworks automatically scale applications based on demand. This means developers do not have to manually adjust server capacity, allowing for better resource utilization.
4. **Enhanced Collaboration**: With configuration files and clear project structures, teams can collaborate more effectively, making it easier to onboard new developers and maintain code quality.
5. **Integration with Cloud Services**: Serverless frameworks often come with built-in support for various cloud services, such as databases, authentication, and messaging queues, allowing for seamless integration and functionality.

Popular Serverless Frameworks

Several serverless frameworks have emerged as leaders in the field, each offering unique features and capabilities. Here are some of the most widely used frameworks:

Serverless Framework

- One of the most popular and widely adopted frameworks, the Serverless Framework allows developers to build and deploy applications on multiple cloud providers, including AWS, Google Cloud, and Azure.
- Features include easy function deployment, support for multiple lan-

guages, and extensive plugin architecture to extend functionality.

- It uses a simple YAML configuration file to define services, functions, and resources, making it straightforward to manage infrastructure as code.

AWS SAM (Serverless Application Model)

- AWS SAM is a framework specifically designed for building serverless applications on AWS. It simplifies the process of defining and deploying AWS Lambda functions and the associated infrastructure.
- SAM uses a special configuration file (template.yaml) to define functions, APIs, and resources, allowing for local testing and debugging.
- It integrates seamlessly with other AWS services, providing a comprehensive toolkit for serverless application development.

Zappa

- Zappa is a lightweight serverless framework specifically for deploying Python applications to AWS Lambda and API Gateway.
- It simplifies the process of deploying Flask and Django applications, providing easy configuration and management of serverless REST APIs.
- Zappa allows developers to focus on writing Python code while handling the complexities of AWS configuration and deployment.

Azure Functions

- Azure Functions is a serverless compute service provided by Microsoft Azure. It allows developers to run event-driven code without provisioning or managing infrastructure.
- With Azure Functions, developers can easily create functions using various programming languages, including Python, C#, and JavaScript.
- Azure Functions integrates seamlessly with other Azure services, enabling the creation of comprehensive serverless solutions.

Google Cloud Functions

- Google Cloud Functions is a serverless execution environment that allows developers to run code in response to events originating from Google Cloud services or HTTP requests.
- It supports multiple languages, including Python, Node.js, and Go, providing flexibility in development.
- Google Cloud Functions integrates with other Google Cloud services, enabling developers to build complex applications quickly.

Choosing the Right Serverless Framework

When selecting a serverless framework, consider the following factors:

- **Cloud Provider**: Some frameworks are optimized for specific cloud providers (e.g., AWS SAM for AWS), while others are multi-cloud (e.g., Serverless Framework).
- **Language Support**: Ensure that the framework supports the programming language you prefer or require for your project.
- **Ecosystem and Community**: Consider the size and activity of the community around the framework. A strong community can provide valuable support, plugins, and extensions.
- **Ease of Use**: Evaluate the documentation, setup process, and learning curve associated with each framework to determine which one aligns best with your development workflow.

Serverless frameworks are essential tools for modern application development, enabling developers to build, deploy, and manage serverless applications efficiently. By abstracting infrastructure management and providing seamless integration with cloud services, these frameworks empower developers to focus on delivering value through their code. As you explore serverless architectures, understanding the available frameworks and their unique features will be crucial in selecting the right tools for your projects.

Choosing the Right Framework

Selecting the right serverless framework is crucial for optimizing your development process and achieving your project goals. The choice often depends on various factors, including your cloud provider preference, programming language, project complexity, and specific features you may require. This section will provide an overview of three popular frameworks: AWS Lambda, Serverless Framework, and Zappa, along with considerations to help you make an informed decision.

AWS Lambda

Overview

AWS Lambda is Amazon's serverless compute service that allows you to run code in response to events without provisioning or managing servers. It automatically scales applications by running code in response to each trigger.

Key Features

- **Event-Driven**: AWS Lambda functions can be triggered by a wide range of AWS services, including S3 (for file uploads), DynamoDB (for database changes), API Gateway (for HTTP requests), and CloudWatch Events.
- **Language Support**: AWS Lambda natively supports multiple programming languages, including Python, Node.js, Java, C#, Ruby, and Go.
- **Integration with AWS Services**: Seamless integration with the AWS ecosystem allows for building robust applications that can leverage other AWS services like RDS, SQS, SNS, and more.
- **Pay-per-Use Pricing**: You are charged based on the number of requests and the duration of code execution, making it cost-effective for variable

workloads.

When to Choose AWS Lambda

- If you are already using AWS for your infrastructure and services.
- If you require tight integration with other AWS services.
- If your application is event-driven and can benefit from automatic scaling.

Serverless Framework
Overview
The Serverless Framework is an open-source framework that allows developers to build and deploy serverless applications across multiple cloud providers, including AWS, Google Cloud Platform, Azure, and others.
Key Features

- **Multi-Cloud Support**: It enables developers to deploy applications on various cloud platforms, providing flexibility to choose the best provider for each project.
- **Configuration as Code**: The framework uses a simple YAML configuration file to define functions, resources, and plugins, making it easy to manage and version control your infrastructure.
- **Extensible via Plugins**: The Serverless Framework has a rich ecosystem of plugins that extend its functionality, allowing for features like monitoring, security, and custom integrations.
- **CLI Tooling**: A powerful command-line interface simplifies deploying, managing, and monitoring serverless applications.

When to Choose Serverless Framework

- If you want the flexibility to deploy on multiple cloud platforms.
- If you prefer a robust plugin system that can enhance your application.
- If you want to manage your infrastructure as code with clear, declarative configurations.

Zappa

Overview

Zappa is a lightweight serverless framework specifically designed for deploying Python web applications to AWS Lambda and API Gateway. It simplifies the process of creating and managing serverless applications using popular web frameworks like Flask and Django.

Key Features

- **Ease of Use**: Zappa automates much of the deployment process, making it straightforward to get Python web applications running on AWS Lambda.
- **Framework Compatibility**: It works seamlessly with Flask and Django, allowing you to leverage the features of these frameworks while deploying to a serverless architecture.
- **Automatic AWS Configuration**: Zappa takes care of creating necessary AWS resources and permissions automatically, simplifying the setup for developers.
- **Local Development**: Zappa includes tools for local testing and debugging, enabling developers to test their applications before deploying.

When to Choose Zappa

- If you are building Python web applications, particularly with Flask or Django.
- If you want a simple setup process for deploying serverless applications on AWS.
- If you prefer focusing on developing your application without extensive infrastructure management.

Choosing the right serverless framework is vital for the success of your application. AWS Lambda is ideal for those deeply integrated into the AWS ecosystem and looking for a robust serverless solution. The Serverless Framework offers flexibility across multiple cloud providers, making it a versatile choice for diverse projects. Zappa shines for Python developers, providing a straightforward path to deploying web applications on AWS Lambda. Assess your project's specific needs, team expertise, and desired features to select the framework that aligns best with your goals.

Creating Your First Serverless Application

Setting Up Your First Function

In this chapter, we will guide you through the process of setting up your first serverless function using AWS Lambda. This step-by-step guide will cover everything from configuring your AWS account to deploying your function, allowing you to gain hands-on experience with serverless architecture.

Prerequisites

Before you begin, ensure you have the following:

1. **AWS Account**: You will need an AWS account to access AWS Lambda and other related services. If you do not have an account, you can sign up at aws.amazon.com.
2. **AWS Management Console**: Familiarity with the AWS Management Console, where you will create and manage your Lambda functions.
3. **Basic Understanding of Python**: This guide will use Python as the programming language for the Lambda function.

Step 1: Log into the AWS Management Console

1. Go to the AWS Management Console.
2. Sign in using your AWS account credentials.

Step 2: Navigate to AWS Lambda

1. In the AWS Management Console, locate the "Services" menu at the top left corner.
2. Under the "Compute" section, click on **Lambda** to open the AWS Lambda dashboard.

Step 3: Create a New Lambda Function

- On the Lambda dashboard, click on the **Create function** button.
- **Select a creation method**:

Choose **Author from scratch**.

- **Configure function settings**:

Function name: Enter a name for your function (e.g., HelloWorldFunction).
Runtime: Select **Python 3.x** (choose the latest version available).
Permissions:
For a simple setup, choose **Create a new role with basic Lambda permissions**. This will create an IAM role that allows your function to write logs to CloudWatch.

- Click on the **Create function** button to proceed.

Step 4: Write Your Lambda Function Code

1. After the function is created, you will be taken to the function configuration page.
2. In the **Function code** section, you will see a built-in code editor.
3. Replace the existing code with the following simple Python code:

```python
python

def lambda_handler(event, context):
    return {
        'statusCode': 200,
        'body': 'Hello, World!'
    }
```

- This function simply returns a message saying "Hello, World!" when it is invoked.

1. Click on the **Deploy** button in the upper right corner to save your changes.

Step 5: Configure a Test Event

1. In the function configuration page, click on the **Test** button.
2. A dialog will appear prompting you to configure a test event.
3. **Create a new test event**:

- **Event name**: Enter a name for your test event (e.g., TestEvent).
- Leave the default JSON event as is. It can be a simple event for our example.

1. Click on the **Create** button.

Step 6: Test Your Lambda Function

1. With your test event created, click on the **Test** button again.
2. The AWS Lambda service will invoke your function using the test event you configured.
3. After execution, you will see the results displayed, including:

- **Execution result**: The output of your function, which should display the message: {"statusCode": 200, "body": "Hello, World!"}
- **Execution duration**: The time taken to execute the function.
- **Logs**: Any logs generated during the execution will be displayed here.

1. If the output is as expected, congratulations! You have successfully created and tested your first AWS Lambda function.

Step 7: Monitor Logs in CloudWatch

1. AWS Lambda automatically integrates with Amazon CloudWatch to provide logging capabilities.
2. To view the logs generated by your function, go to the **Monitoring** tab in your function's configuration page.
3. Click on **View logs in CloudWatch** to open the CloudWatch Logs console.
4. You can select the log stream corresponding to your function executions to see detailed logs, including any print statements or errors.

Step 8: Clean Up Resources

To avoid incurring charges on your AWS account, it's good practice to delete resources you no longer need.

1. Return to the AWS Lambda dashboard.
2. Select your function (e.g., HelloWorldFunction).
3. Click on the **Actions** button, then choose **Delete function** to remove your Lambda function.

Setting up your first function in AWS Lambda is a straightforward process that introduces you to the serverless paradigm. By creating a simple "Hello, World!" function, you have learned how to configure AWS Lambda, write function code, test it, and monitor its execution through CloudWatch. This foundational knowledge will serve as the basis for developing more complex serverless applications as you continue your journey into serverless computing with Python.

Understanding Event Sources

In a serverless architecture, event sources are the triggers that initiate the execution of serverless functions, such as those in AWS Lambda. Understanding how these event sources work is essential for designing responsive and efficient applications. This section will explore the various types of event sources, their significance, and how they integrate with serverless functions.

What Are Event Sources?

Event sources are external systems or services that generate events, which can be used to trigger the execution of a serverless function. These events can originate from various sources, such as user interactions, changes in data, system notifications, or scheduled events. In the context of AWS Lambda, event sources can be AWS services or external systems that invoke the function based on specific conditions or actions.

Types of Event Sources

Here are some common types of event sources that can trigger AWS Lambda functions:

1. HTTP Requests via API Gateway

- **Overview**: API Gateway allows developers to create RESTful APIs that can invoke Lambda functions in response to HTTP requests.
- **Use Cases**: This is commonly used to build web applications, mobile backends, and microservices that require a serverless API.

- **Integration**: When an API Gateway receives an HTTP request, it forwards the request data as an event to the associated Lambda function, which processes the request and returns a response.

2. AWS S3 (Simple Storage Service)

- **Overview**: AWS S3 is a cloud storage service that can trigger Lambda functions in response to specific actions, such as file uploads, deletions, or modifications.
- **Use Cases**: This is often used for processing images, video files, data uploads, or any kind of object that requires immediate handling once it is uploaded.
- **Integration**: When an object is created or deleted in an S3 bucket, the corresponding event is sent to the Lambda function, allowing for automated processing or notifications.

3. AWS DynamoDB

- **Overview**: DynamoDB is a fully managed NoSQL database service that can trigger Lambda functions in response to changes in the data.
- **Use Cases**: This is useful for applications that require real-time data processing, such as logging, notifications, or triggering workflows based on data changes.
- **Integration**: DynamoDB Streams capture changes to items in a table, and these changes can be sent as events to Lambda functions for processing.

4. AWS CloudWatch Events

- **Overview**: CloudWatch Events allow you to respond to system events, such as scheduled events or changes in AWS resources.
- **Use Cases**: This is commonly used for automated tasks, such as running maintenance jobs, cleaning up resources, or responding to specific operational changes.

- **Integration**: You can configure CloudWatch Events to invoke Lambda functions on a schedule (using cron expressions) or in response to specific AWS service events.

5. AWS SNS (Simple Notification Service)

- **Overview**: AWS SNS is a messaging service that enables you to send notifications and messages to multiple subscribers.
- **Use Cases**: SNS is often used for application alerts, user notifications, or any scenario where messages need to be distributed to multiple recipients.
- **Integration**: You can configure SNS topics to trigger Lambda functions when messages are published to those topics, allowing for real-time processing of notifications.

6. AWS SQS (Simple Queue Service)

- **Overview**: AWS SQS is a message queuing service that allows for decoupling of components in a distributed application.
- **Use Cases**: SQS is used for asynchronous communication between microservices or components that may not operate at the same speed.
- **Integration**: Lambda can poll SQS queues and invoke functions to process messages as they arrive, ensuring that tasks are handled in a scalable manner.

7. Custom Event Sources

- **Overview**: You can create custom applications or services that generate events for your Lambda functions to process.
- **Use Cases**: This is beneficial for unique workflows or integration with third-party services that provide webhook capabilities.
- **Integration**: Custom applications can invoke Lambda functions directly via API calls, passing event data as needed.

Best Practices for Using Event Sources

1. **Choose the Right Event Source**: Consider the nature of your application and its requirements when selecting event sources. For example, use API Gateway for HTTP requests, S3 for file uploads, and DynamoDB for data-driven events.

2. **Monitor and Manage Events**: Utilize AWS CloudWatch to monitor the invocation of your functions and set up alerts for error handling. This will help you manage performance and identify issues quickly.

3. **Handle Events Efficiently**: Ensure your Lambda functions are optimized for the type and frequency of events they will handle. Use batching or asynchronous processing when working with SQS or DynamoDB Streams to improve performance.

4. **Consider Security and Permissions**: Make sure that the IAM roles and policies associated with your Lambda functions have the necessary permissions to access the event sources they are designed to interact with.

5. **Test Event Sources Thoroughly**: Before deploying your application, test your Lambda functions with the associated event sources to ensure that everything works as expected and that the event handling is robust.

Understanding event sources is fundamental to leveraging the full power of serverless architecture. By knowing how various AWS services and external systems can trigger your Lambda functions, you can design responsive, efficient, and scalable applications. As you continue your journey in serverless development, mastering event sources will enable you to build sophisticated workflows that react to changes and events in real time.

Real-World Projects

Project 1: Simple Web Application

I n this project, we will create a simple web application using AWS Lambda and API Gateway. The application will be a basic RESTful API that responds to HTTP requests, demonstrating how to leverage server less architecture for web development. This project will cover the entire process from setup to deployment, allowing you to gain practical experience with server less frameworks.

Overview of the Web Application

The goal of this project is to build a simple API that provides a greeting message. The application will have the following endpoints:

- **GET /greet**: Returns a greeting message.
- **POST /greet**: Accepts a name as input and returns a personalized greeting message.

This application will demonstrate how to create a serverless backend that can handle both GET and POST requests.

Prerequisites

Before starting this project, ensure you have the following:

1. An active AWS account with access to AWS Lambda and API Gateway.

2. Basic knowledge of Python programming.
3. Familiarity with the AWS Management Console.

Step 1: Create a New Lambda Function

1. **Log into the AWS Management Console** and navigate to AWS Lambda.
2. Click on the **Create function** button.
3. **Choose "Author from scratch".**
4. **Configure the function settings**:

- **Function name**: Enter GreetingFunction.
- **Runtime**: Select **Python 3.x.**
- **Permissions**: Choose **Create a new role with basic Lambda permissions.**

1. Click **Create function.**

Step 2: Write the Function Code

1. In the **Function code** section, replace the default code with the following Python code:

```python
import json

def lambda_handler(event, context):
    if event['httpMethod'] == 'GET':
        return {
            'statusCode': 200,
            'body': json.dumps('Hello, World!')
        }
```

```
elif event['httpMethod'] == 'POST':
    body = json.loads(event['body'])
    name = body.get('name', 'World')
    return {
        'statusCode': 200,
        'body': json.dumps(f'Hello, {name}!')
    }
else:
    return {
        'statusCode': 400,
        'body': json.dumps('Unsupported method')
    }
```

- This code defines a Lambda function that handles both GET and POST requests. For a GET request, it returns a simple greeting. For a POST request, it retrieves the name from the request body and returns a personalized greeting.

1. Click on the **Deploy** button to save your changes.

Step 3: Set Up API Gateway

1. **Navigate to API Gateway** in the AWS Management Console.
2. Click on **Create API** and choose **REST API** (not private).
3. **Configure the API settings**:

- **API name**: Enter GreetingAPI.
- **Endpoint Type**: Select **Regional**.

1. Click **Create API**.

Step 4: Create Resource and Methods

1. **Create a Resource**:

- In the API Gateway console, select your API.
- Click on **Actions** and choose **Create Resource**.
- **Resource Name**: Enter greet.
- **Resource Path**: This will automatically populate.
- Click **Create Resource**.

1. **Create GET Method**:

- Select the greet resource.
- Click on **Actions** and choose **Create Method**.
- Select **GET** from the dropdown and click the checkmark.
- **Integration Type**: Select **Lambda Function**.
- **Lambda Function**: Enter GreetingFunction.
- Click **Save**, and when prompted, grant API Gateway permission to invoke your Lambda function.

1. **Create POST Method**:

- With the greet resource selected, click on **Actions** and choose **Create Method**.
- Select **POST** from the dropdown and click the checkmark.
- Repeat the integration steps as you did for the GET method, ensuring it points to the same GreetingFunction.
- Click **Save**.

Step 5: Deploy the API

1. Click on **Actions** and select **Deploy API**.
2. **Deployment Stage**:

- **Stage name**: Enter dev.
- Click **Deploy**.

1. Note the **Invoke URL** provided after deployment. This URL will be used to access your API.

Step 6: Test the API

Test the GET Method:

- Open a web browser or a tool like Postman.
- Enter the GET endpoint: https://<your-api-id>.execute-api.<region>.a mazonaws.com/dev/greet.
- You should see the response: {"message": "Hello, World!"}.

Test the POST Method:

- In Postman, set the method to POST and enter the endpoint: https://<y our-api-id>.execute-api.<region>.amazonaws.com/dev/greet.
- In the body, select **raw** and choose **JSON** format. Enter the following:

```json
{
    "name": "Alice"
}
```

- Click **Send**. You should see the response: {"message": "Hello, Alice!"}.

Step 7: Monitor and Debug

1. To monitor the usage and performance of your Lambda function, navigate to the **Monitoring** tab in the Lambda console.
2. You can also check the CloudWatch logs for detailed execution information by clicking on **View logs in CloudWatch**.

Step 8: Clean Up Resources

To avoid unnecessary charges, it's good practice to delete resources you no longer need:

1. Go to the API Gateway console, select your API (GreetingAPI), and click on **Actions > Delete API**.
2. Navigate to the Lambda console, select your function (GreetingFunction), and click on **Actions > Delete function**.

In this project, you have successfully created a simple web application using AWS Lambda and API Gateway. By building a RESTful API that responds to GET and POST requests, you gained hands-on experience with serverless architecture. This foundational project demonstrates the power and simplicity of serverless applications and sets the stage for more complex projects as you continue your journey in serverless development.

Project 2: Data Processing Pipeline

In this project, we will create a data processing pipeline using AWS Lambda, AWS S3, and AWS DynamoDB. The pipeline will automatically process incoming data files stored in an S3 bucket, extract relevant information, and store it in a DynamoDB table for further analysis. This project will demonstrate how to build a robust serverless architecture for handling data ingestion and processing.

Overview of the Data Processing Pipeline

The goal of this project is to set up a pipeline that performs the following tasks:

1. A file is uploaded to an S3 bucket.
2. An AWS Lambda function is triggered by the S3 upload event.
3. The Lambda function processes the file, extracting relevant data.
4. The extracted data is stored in a DynamoDB table.

This application will showcase how to integrate multiple AWS services to create an automated data processing solution.

Prerequisites

Before starting this project, ensure you have the following:

1. An active AWS account with access to AWS Lambda, S3, and DynamoDB.
2. Basic knowledge of Python programming.
3. Familiarity with the AWS Management Console.

Step 1: Set Up the S3 Bucket

1. **Log into the AWS Management Console** and navigate to S3.
2. Click on **Create bucket**.
3. **Configure bucket settings**:

- **Bucket name**: Enter a unique name (e.g., my-data-processing-bucket).
- **Region**: Choose the region where you want to create the bucket.
- Leave other settings as default for this project.

1. Click **Create bucket**.

Step 2: Create a DynamoDB Table

1. **Navigate to DynamoDB** in the AWS Management Console.
2. Click on **Create table**.
3. **Configure table settings**:

- **Table name**: Enter ProcessedData.
- **Primary key**: Set id as the partition key with type **String**.

1. Leave other settings as default and click **Create table**.

Step 3: Create the Lambda Function

1. **Navigate to AWS Lambda** in the AWS Management Console.
2. Click on **Create function**.
3. **Choose "Author from scratch"**.
4. **Configure function settings**:

- **Function name**: Enter DataProcessingFunction.
- **Runtime**: Select **Python 3.x**.
- **Permissions**: Choose **Create a new role with basic Lambda permissions**.

1. Click **Create function**.

Step 4: Write the Lambda Function Code

1. In the **Function code** section, replace the default code with the following Python code:

```python
python

import json
import boto3

s3_client = boto3.client('s3')
dynamodb = boto3.resource('dynamodb')
table = dynamodb.Table('ProcessedData')

def lambda_handler(event, context):
    # Get the bucket name and object key from the event
    bucket = event['Records'][0]['s3']['bucket']['name']
    key = event['Records'][0]['s3']['object']['key']

    # Retrieve the file from S3
    response = s3_client.get_object(Bucket=bucket, Key=key)
    data = response['Body'].read().decode('utf-8')

    # Process the data (for example, we will assume it's CSV)
    lines = data.splitlines()
    for line in lines:
        # Here we assume the line is in CSV format
        fields = line.split(',')
        # Create a unique ID for each record (in practice, use a
        better method)
        record_id = fields[0]  # Assume the first field is a
        unique ID
        # Store the record in DynamoDB
        table.put_item(Item={
            'id': record_id,
            'field1': fields[1],
            'field2': fields[2],
        })
```

```
return {
    'statusCode': 200,
    'body': json.dumps('Data processed successfully')
}
```

- This code defines a Lambda function that retrieves a CSV file from S3, processes each line, and stores the relevant data in a DynamoDB table.

1. Click on the **Deploy** button to save your changes.

Step 5: Set Up S3 Event Notification

1. Go back to your S3 bucket (my-data-processing-bucket).
2. Select the bucket and go to the **Properties** tab.
3. Scroll down to **Event notifications** and click on **Create event notification**.
4. **Configure event notification**:

- **Event name**: Enter ProcessDataEvent.
- **Event types**: Select **All object create events**.
- **Destination**: Choose **Lambda function** and select DataProcessingFunction.

1. Click **Save changes**.

Step 6: Test the Data Processing Pipeline

1. Create a sample CSV file to test the pipeline. The file should have the following format:

```bash
bash

id,field1,field2
1,Hello,World
2,AWS,Serverless
3,Data,Processing
```

1. Upload the CSV file to your S3 bucket (my-data-processing-bucket).
2. After the file is uploaded, the Lambda function will be triggered automatically.

Step 7: Verify Data in DynamoDB

1. **Navigate to DynamoDB** in the AWS Management Console.
2. Select the ProcessedData table.
3. Click on the **Items** tab to view the records stored in the table.
4. You should see the entries corresponding to the data processed from your CSV file.

Step 8: Monitor and Debug

1. To monitor the usage and performance of your Lambda function, navigate to the **Monitoring** tab in the Lambda console.
2. Check CloudWatch logs for detailed execution information. You can access the logs by clicking on **View logs in CloudWatch**.

Step 9: Clean Up Resources

To avoid unnecessary charges, it's good practice to delete resources you no longer need:

1. Go to the S3 console, select your bucket (my-data-processing-bucket), and click on **Delete bucket**.

2. Navigate to the DynamoDB console, select your table (ProcessedData), and click on **Delete**.

3. Return to the Lambda console, select your function (DataProcessingFu nction), and click on **Actions > Delete function**.

In this project, you have successfully created a data processing pipeline using AWS Lambda, S3, and DynamoDB. By building a serverless application that automatically processes files uploaded to S3 and stores the extracted data in DynamoDB, you have demonstrated the power and efficiency of serverless architecture for handling data ingestion and processing. This foundational knowledge will enable you to develop more complex data-driven applications as you advance in your serverless journey.

API Management

Building APIs with AWS API Gateway

AWS API Gateway is a fully managed service that simplifies the creation, deployment, and management of APIs at any scale. It provides a robust platform for building RESTful and WebSocket APIs that can integrate with various AWS services, including AWS Lambda, DynamoDB, and more. This chapter will provide a comprehensive overview of AWS API Gateway, covering its features, benefits, and step-by-step guidance on building and deploying APIs.

Overview of AWS API Gateway

AWS API Gateway allows developers to create APIs that serve as a gateway to backend services. It offers capabilities to manage traffic, enforce security, and provide analytics for API usage. With API Gateway, you can create REST APIs, which use HTTP requests to send and receive data, and WebSocket APIs, which enable two-way communication between clients and servers.

Key Features of AWS API Gateway:

- **Support for RESTful APIs**: Create and manage RESTful APIs that conform to REST principles, enabling seamless integration with web applications and mobile clients.
- **Integration with AWS Services**: API Gateway can easily connect to AWS Lambda, EC2, DynamoDB, S3, and other AWS services, allowing

you to build serverless applications.

- **Security Features**: Provides built-in security measures, including authentication, authorization (using AWS IAM and Amazon Cognito), and SSL/TLS encryption.
- **Throttling and Caching**: Implement throttling to control API traffic and use caching to reduce latency and improve performance.
- **Monitoring and Analytics**: Integrate with Amazon CloudWatch to monitor API usage, performance metrics, and error logging.

Benefits of Using AWS API Gateway

1. **Scalability**: API Gateway automatically scales to accommodate varying levels of traffic, ensuring consistent performance without the need for manual intervention.
2. **Cost-Effective**: With a pay-as-you-go pricing model, you only pay for the API calls made and the data transferred out, making it a cost-effective solution for managing APIs.
3. **Reduced Operational Overhead**: As a fully managed service, API Gateway eliminates the need to manage servers, allowing you to focus on building and deploying your applications.
4. **Flexible Deployment Options**: Deploy APIs to multiple stages (e.g., development, testing, production) and easily roll back to previous versions if necessary.
5. **Custom Domain Names**: Support for custom domain names, allowing you to create branded API endpoints that are easy for developers to remember and use.

Step-by-Step Guide to Building APIs with AWS API Gateway

In this section, we will walk through the process of building a simple RESTful API using AWS API Gateway and AWS Lambda. Our example API will provide a greeting message and accept a name parameter for personalized responses.

Step 1: Set Up Your Lambda Function

1. **Log into the AWS Management Console** and navigate to AWS Lambda.
2. Click on **Create function**.
3. **Choose "Author from scratch"**.
4. **Configure function settings**:

- **Function name**: Enter GreetingFunction.
- **Runtime**: Select **Python 3.x**.
- **Permissions**: Choose **Create a new role with basic Lambda permissions**.

1. Click **Create function**.
2. In the **Function code** section, add the following Python code:

```python
import json

def lambda_handler(event, context):
    name = event.get('queryStringParameters', {}).get('name',
    'World')
    message = f"Hello, {name}!"

    return {
        'statusCode': 200,
        'body': json.dumps({'message': message})
    }
```

1. Click on the **Deploy** button to save your changes.

Step 2: Create an API in API Gateway

1. **Navigate to API Gateway** in the AWS Management Console.
2. Click on **Create API** and choose **REST API** (not private).

3. **Configure API settings**:

- **API name**: Enter GreetingAPI.
- **Endpoint Type**: Select **Regional**.

1. Click **Create API**.

Step 3: Create a Resource

1. In the API Gateway console, select your newly created API.
2. Click on **Actions** and choose **Create Resource**.
3. **Configure resource settings**:

- **Resource Name**: Enter greet.
- **Resource Path**: This will automatically populate.

1. Click **Create Resource**.

Step 4: Create a GET Method

1. With the greet resource selected, click on **Actions** and choose **Create Method**.
2. Select **GET** from the dropdown and click the checkmark.
3. **Integration Type**: Select **Lambda Function**.
4. **Lambda Function**: Enter GreetingFunction.
5. Click **Save** and grant API Gateway permission to invoke your Lambda function when prompted.

Step 5: Enable CORS (Cross-Origin Resource Sharing)

1. Select the **GET** method under the greet resource.
2. Click on **Enable CORS** from the Actions dropdown.
3. Leave the default settings and click **Enable CORS and replace existing**

CORS headers.

4. Confirm the changes.

Step 6: Deploy the API

1. Click on **Actions** and select **Deploy API**.
2. **Deployment Stage**:

- **Stage name**: Enter dev.

1. Click **Deploy**.
2. Note the **Invoke URL** provided after deployment. This URL will be used to access your API.

Step 7: Test the API

1. Open a web browser or a tool like Postman.
2. For a personalized greeting, enter the following URL in the browser or Postman:

```php
https://<your-api-id>.execute-api
.<region>.amazonaws.com/dev/greet?name=Alice
```

- You should receive a response similar to:

```json
{
    "message": "Hello, Alice!"
}
```

```
}
```

1. To test the default response, enter:

```php
https://<your-api-id>.execute-api.
<region>.amazonaws.com/dev/greet
```

- You should receive:

```json
{
  "message": "Hello, World!"
}
```

Step 8: Monitor and Manage Your API

1. **Monitoring**: Navigate to the **Monitoring** tab in the API Gateway console to view metrics such as latency, request counts, and error rates.
2. **CloudWatch Logs**: Enable logging to capture request and response data for further analysis and debugging.

Step 9: Clean Up Resources

To avoid unnecessary charges, it's good practice to delete resources you no longer need:

1. Go to the API Gateway console, select your API (GreetingAPI), and click on **Actions > Delete API**.
2. Navigate to the Lambda console, select your function (GreetingFunc-

tion), and click on **Actions > Delete function**.

In this section, you have successfully built a RESTful API using AWS API Gateway and AWS Lambda. By creating a simple greeting API, you demonstrated the capabilities of API Gateway to manage HTTP requests and integrate with Lambda functions. Understanding how to build APIs is a fundamental skill in developing serverless applications, enabling you to create scalable, efficient, and easily managed backends for your applications. As you continue to explore API management, you can enhance your APIs with additional features such as authentication, rate limiting, and documentation, paving the way for more complex and robust applications.

Integrating with Other Services

Integrating AWS API Gateway with other AWS services is essential for building comprehensive serverless applications. This integration allows you to leverage various AWS resources, such as databases, storage solutions, and authentication services, to create powerful, scalable, and responsive applications. In this section, we will explore some common integrations, the benefits they provide, and how to implement them in your serverless architecture.

Common Integrations with AWS API Gateway

1. **AWS Lambda**

- **Overview**: As previously discussed, AWS Lambda is often the primary backend for APIs created with API Gateway. It allows you to run code in response to API requests without provisioning servers.

- **Implementation**: When you create an API method in API Gateway, you can directly link it to a Lambda function. The function processes incoming requests and returns responses.
- **Use Case**: Building a serverless RESTful API where the business logic is encapsulated in Lambda functions.

1. **AWS DynamoDB**

- **Overview**: DynamoDB is a fully managed NoSQL database that can store and retrieve any amount of data with low latency. It is an excellent choice for serverless applications due to its scalability and performance.
- **Implementation**: You can configure your Lambda function to perform CRUD (Create, Read, Update, Delete) operations on DynamoDB tables based on API requests.
- **Use Case**: Creating a serverless application that requires data storage, such as a user management system or inventory tracker.

1. **Amazon S3**

- **Overview**: Amazon S3 is a scalable object storage service commonly used for storing static files, images, and backups.
- **Implementation**: You can configure API Gateway to trigger Lambda functions that interact with S3, such as uploading files or processing images stored in S3 buckets.
- **Use Case**: Developing an image upload service where users can submit images via the API, and the application processes and stores them in S3.

1. **Amazon RDS**

- **Overview**: Amazon RDS (Relational Database Service) provides managed relational databases, such as MySQL, PostgreSQL, and SQL Server.
- **Implementation**: Integrate API Gateway with Lambda functions that

connect to an RDS database for executing SQL queries in response to API requests.

- **Use Case**: Building a serverless web application that requires structured data storage, such as a content management system (CMS).

1. AWS Step Functions

- **Overview**: AWS Step Functions is a serverless orchestration service that enables you to coordinate multiple AWS services into serverless workflows.
- **Implementation**: Use API Gateway to trigger Step Functions state machines, allowing you to manage complex workflows that include multiple Lambda functions and other services.
- **Use Case**: Orchestrating a multi-step process, such as processing an order in an e-commerce application.

1. Amazon Cognito

- **Overview**: Amazon Cognito provides user authentication, authorization, and user management for web and mobile apps.
- **Implementation**: Configure API Gateway to require authentication via Cognito User Pools, ensuring that only authenticated users can access certain API endpoints.
- **Use Case**: Protecting sensitive API resources, such as user data or admin functionalities, by implementing user authentication and authorization.

Step-by-Step Guide to Integrate API Gateway with AWS Lambda and DynamoDB

In this example, we will extend the previous greeting API to store and retrieve personalized greetings using DynamoDB.

Step 1: Update the Lambda Function

1. Go to the AWS Lambda console and select your GreetingFunction.

2. Update the function code to include DynamoDB interactions:

```python
import json
import boto3

dynamodb = boto3.resource('dynamodb')
table = dynamodb.Table('ProcessedData')

def lambda_handler(event, context):
    if event['httpMethod'] == 'GET':
        name = event.get('queryStringParameters', {}).get('name',
        'World')
        return {
            'statusCode': 200,
            'body': json.dumps({'message': f'Hello, {name}!'})
        }
    elif event['httpMethod'] == 'POST':
        body = json.loads(event['body'])
        name = body.get('name', 'World')
        # Store the greeting in DynamoDB
        table.put_item(Item={'name': name, 'greeting': f'Hello,
        {name}!'})
        return {
            'statusCode': 200,
            'body': json.dumps({'message': f'Hello, {name}!'})
        }
    else:
        return {
            'statusCode': 400,
            'body': json.dumps('Unsupported method')
        }
```

1. Click **Deploy** to save your changes.

Step 2: Update the DynamoDB Table

1. Navigate to the DynamoDB console and select your ProcessedData table.
2. Ensure the table has a primary key set to name (String). If not, create a new table with the appropriate schema.

Step 3: Test the Integration

1. Test the POST Method:

- Use Postman or a similar tool to send a POST request to your API endpoint:

```php
https://<your-api-id>.execute-api
.<region>.amazonaws.com/dev/greet
```

- In the body, enter:

```json
{
    "name": "Alice"
}
```

- You should receive a response indicating the greeting has been stored in DynamoDB.

1. Test the GET Method:

- Use Postman or a browser to send a GET request:

```php
https://<your-api-id>.execute-api.
<region>.amazonaws.
com/dev/greet?name=Alice
```

- You should receive the greeting message in response.

Step 4: Monitor and Validate Data in DynamoDB

1. Go to the DynamoDB console and select the ProcessedData table.
2. Click on the **Items** tab to view the records. You should see entries corresponding to the names you've submitted through the API.

Integrating AWS API Gateway with other AWS services such as Lambda and DynamoDB enables you to build powerful, data-driven applications with minimal operational overhead. By following the steps in this section, you have learned how to extend a simple API to interact with a DynamoDB table, showcasing the potential of serverless architecture for creating robust applications. As you continue to explore AWS services, consider how these integrations can enhance your applications, improve user experience, and enable complex workflows.

Monitoring and Debugging

Monitoring Tools Overview

Effective monitoring and debugging are critical components of maintaining robust and reliable serverless applications. AWS provides several powerful tools to help developers monitor application performance, track resource usage, and identify issues. In this section, we will explore **AWS CloudWatch**, the primary monitoring service within the AWS ecosystem, and how it integrates with serverless architecture.

What is AWS CloudWatch?

AWS CloudWatch is a monitoring and observability service that provides data and insights into your AWS resources and applications. It allows you to collect and track metrics, monitor log files, set alarms, and automate actions based on predefined conditions. CloudWatch provides a unified view of your application performance and operational health, making it easier to detect anomalies, troubleshoot issues, and ensure your applications are running smoothly.

Key Features of AWS CloudWatch

Metrics Collection

- CloudWatch collects and stores metrics for AWS resources, allowing you to monitor performance over time.

- Metrics can include CPU utilization, memory usage, request counts, error rates, and custom application metrics.

Logs Management

- CloudWatch Logs enables you to monitor, store, and access log files generated by AWS services, including Lambda functions, EC2 instances, and more.
- You can search and filter logs in real-time to diagnose issues quickly.

Alarms and Notifications

- You can set up CloudWatch Alarms to trigger notifications based on specific thresholds for metrics.
- Alarms can send notifications through Amazon SNS (Simple Notification Service), trigger Lambda functions, or perform automated actions.

Dashboards

- CloudWatch Dashboards provide a customizable interface for visualizing metrics and logs in one place.
- You can create graphs, charts, and widgets to monitor key performance indicators (KPIs) and application health.

Events and Automation

- CloudWatch Events allow you to respond to changes in your AWS environment by triggering actions based on specific events.
- You can automate workflows by invoking Lambda functions, sending notifications, or updating resources in response to events.

Integration with Other AWS Services

- CloudWatch seamlessly integrates with other AWS services, providing comprehensive monitoring across your entire architecture.
- You can monitor resources like RDS databases, S3 buckets, and API Gateway endpoints in addition to Lambda functions.

How AWS CloudWatch Works

1. **Data Collection**: AWS services automatically send performance and operational metrics to CloudWatch. Additionally, you can publish custom metrics from your applications or scripts to monitor specific aspects of your architecture.
2. **Logs Streaming**: Logs from AWS services are streamed to CloudWatch Logs, where they can be analyzed and monitored in real-time. You can also create log groups and log streams to organize and manage your log data effectively.
3. **Alarms Configuration**: You can set alarms based on specific metrics or log events. When an alarm is triggered, CloudWatch can take automated actions, such as sending a notification or scaling resources.
4. **Visualization and Reporting**: CloudWatch Dashboards allow you to visualize key metrics and logs in a single view, enabling you to quickly assess the state of your applications and resources.

Setting Up Monitoring with AWS CloudWatch

To effectively monitor your serverless applications using AWS CloudWatch, follow these steps:

Step 1: Monitor Lambda Function Metrics

1. Navigate to the AWS Lambda console.
2. Select your Lambda function.
3. Click on the **Monitoring** tab to view built-in metrics, including invocation count, duration, error count, and throttles.
4. Use the graphs to analyze trends and performance over time.

Step 2: Set Up CloudWatch Logs for Lambda Functions

1. CloudWatch Logs are automatically created for your Lambda functions when logging is enabled.
2. In your Lambda function code, use the print() function to output logs. These logs will be captured in CloudWatch Logs automatically.

```python
python

def lambda_handler(event, context):
    print("Received event: " + json.dumps(event))
    # Additional processing
```

1. Navigate to the CloudWatch Logs console to view and analyze the log streams generated by your Lambda function.

Step 3: Create Alarms for Performance Metrics

1. In the CloudWatch console, navigate to **Alarms** and click on **Create Alarm**.
2. Choose the metric you want to monitor (e.g., error count, duration) and click **Select metric**.
3. Configure the alarm settings:

- Set the threshold for when the alarm should trigger.
- Choose actions (e.g., send notifications via SNS or trigger another Lambda function) when the alarm state changes.

Step 4: Build Dashboards for Visual Monitoring

1. In the CloudWatch console, navigate to **Dashboards** and click on **Create dashboard**.

2. Name your dashboard and select **Add widget** to visualize your metrics.
3. Choose the type of widget (e.g., line graph, number) and select the metrics you want to display.
4. Save your dashboard to monitor key performance indicators at a glance.

Best Practices for Monitoring and Debugging

1. **Enable Detailed Monitoring**: For critical services, enable detailed monitoring to capture more granular metrics, allowing for better performance insights.
2. **Set Up Notifications**: Configure alarms and notifications for important metrics to proactively manage performance issues and receive alerts before they escalate.
3. **Regularly Review Logs**: Make it a habit to review CloudWatch Logs regularly to identify potential issues, optimize performance, and ensure your application behaves as expected.
4. **Use Structured Logging**: Implement structured logging in your applications, making it easier to parse and analyze logs for specific data points.
5. **Monitor Costs**: Keep an eye on CloudWatch costs, especially if you have numerous custom metrics or logs. Optimize your monitoring strategy to ensure cost-effectiveness.

AWS CloudWatch is an invaluable tool for monitoring and debugging serverless applications built on AWS. By providing comprehensive metrics, logs, and alarm capabilities, CloudWatch empowers developers to maintain high availability and performance while ensuring quick responses to issues. Understanding how to leverage CloudWatch effectively will enhance your ability to build robust serverless applications that meet user expectations and business needs. As you continue to develop and refine your applications, using CloudWatch as a monitoring and debugging tool will be essential for ongoing success.

Debugging Techniques and Best Practices

Debugging serverless applications can be challenging due to the distributed nature of the architecture and the stateless behavior of serverless functions. However, with the right techniques and best practices, you can effectively identify and resolve issues in your AWS Lambda functions and other integrated services. This section explores various debugging techniques and best practices to enhance your debugging process.

Debugging Techniques

Utilize CloudWatch Logs

Log Outputs: Use print() statements in your Lambda functions to output relevant information at various stages of execution. This can help you trace the flow of data and identify where things may be going wrong.

Structured Logging: Implement structured logging (using JSON format) to make it easier to search and analyze log entries. This allows you to filter logs based on specific attributes, making it more efficient to locate issues.

Log Level Management: Implement different log levels (e.g., DEBUG, INFO, WARNING, ERROR) to control the verbosity of your logs. This helps capture detailed information during development and testing while minimizing log output in production.

Use AWS X-Ray for Tracing

Overview: AWS X-Ray is a distributed tracing service that helps you analyze and debug microservices applications, providing insights into performance bottlenecks and error rates.

Integration with Lambda: You can enable X-Ray tracing for your Lambda functions, allowing you to visualize the request flow and identify latencies in your application.

Service Map: X-Ray generates a service map that visually represents the relationships and latency between your services, making it easier to diagnose issues.

Test Locally Before Deployment

Local Testing: Use tools like AWS SAM (Serverless Application Model) or the Serverless Framework to run your Lambda functions locally. This allows you to simulate events and test functionality without deploying to AWS.

Unit Testing: Implement unit tests using frameworks like unittest or pytest in Python to validate individual components of your code. This helps catch errors early in the development process.

Utilize API Gateway Test Features

Test Your API Endpoints: API Gateway provides built-in test features that allow you to simulate requests and verify the responses from your Lambda functions.

View Logs: When you test your API endpoints, you can view the logs generated in CloudWatch to check for any errors or unexpected behavior.

Error Handling in Lambda Functions

Try-Except Blocks: Use try-except blocks to handle exceptions gracefully within your Lambda functions. This can prevent unhandled exceptions from causing your function to fail and allow you to return meaningful error messages.

Custom Error Responses: Design your function to return custom error responses for different scenarios, providing clarity to the client about what went wrong.

Best Practices for Debugging Serverless Applications

Implement Comprehensive Monitoring

Regularly monitor metrics and logs through CloudWatch to gain insights into function performance and health. Set up alerts for critical metrics (e.g., error rates, duration) to proactively address issues.

Maintain Clear Documentation

Document your code thoroughly, including the purpose of functions, expected inputs, and outputs. Clear documentation makes it easier for team members to understand the logic and identify issues.

Adopt a Consistent Naming Convention

Use consistent naming conventions for your Lambda functions, environment variables, and resources. This reduces confusion and makes it easier to identify the purpose of each component during debugging.

Embrace Version Control and CI/CD

Utilize version control systems (e.g., Git) to manage your codebase effectively. Implement CI/CD pipelines to automate testing and deployment, ensuring that only thoroughly tested code is released.

Perform Regular Code Reviews

Conduct code reviews as part of your development process. Fresh eyes can catch potential issues and provide suggestions for improvement, enhancing code quality and reducing the likelihood of bugs.

Utilize Feature Flags

Implement feature flags to control the rollout of new features. This allows you to deploy code without exposing new functionality to users until you are ready, reducing the risk of introducing bugs.

Backup and Rollback Strategies

Maintain a backup of your configuration and code. Develop rollback strategies to quickly revert to previous stable versions if issues arise in production.

Debugging serverless applications requires a combination of effective techniques and best practices to ensure reliability and performance. By leveraging tools like AWS CloudWatch and AWS X-Ray, implementing structured logging, and adhering to best practices for monitoring and testing, you can enhance your debugging process and maintain robust serverless applications. As you continue to develop your skills in serverless architecture, remember that a proactive and organized approach to debugging will greatly contribute to your success in building scalable and efficient applications.

Advanced Concepts

Event-Driven Architecture

E vent-driven architecture (EDA) is a design pattern in which applications are built around the production, detection, consumption, and reaction to events. This architectural approach is particularly well-suited for serverless applications, allowing for highly decoupled systems that can scale efficiently and respond to changes in real time. This section explores the principles of event-driven architecture, its components, benefits, and practical implementations in the context of serverless computing.

What is Event-Driven Architecture?

Event-driven architecture focuses on the communication between components through events, which are significant changes in state or occurrences within a system. In an EDA, components are designed to react to events rather than relying on direct calls to one another. This allows for greater flexibility, scalability, and responsiveness in application design.

Key concepts include:

- **Event**: An event is a significant change in state or an occurrence that is generated by a producer (e.g., a user action, a system change, or a scheduled task).
- **Event Producer**: The component or service that generates events. This can be anything from a user interface action to a change in a database.

- **Event Consumer**: The component or service that listens for events and takes action in response. Consumers can react to events by executing business logic, triggering workflows, or updating state.
- **Event Broker**: A middleware component that facilitates the communication between event producers and consumers. It manages the delivery of events and can provide features like message filtering, routing, and persistence.

Components of Event-Driven Architecture

Event Producers Producers generate events that indicate a change in state or an occurrence within the system. In a serverless context, this could be an AWS Lambda function, an IoT device, or an external application sending data.

Event Consumers Consumers are services or applications that react to events. They perform operations based on the event's content, such as processing data, updating databases, or triggering additional workflows.

Event Broker The event broker is responsible for delivering events from producers to consumers. It can handle message queuing, topic subscriptions, and event filtering. Common AWS services that serve as event brokers include:

- **Amazon SNS (Simple Notification Service)**: A pub/sub messaging service that allows you to send messages to multiple subscribers.
- **Amazon SQS (Simple Queue Service)**: A message queuing service that enables decoupling of components by allowing messages to be stored and processed asynchronously.
- **Amazon EventBridge**: A serverless event bus service that connects applications using events from AWS services, integrated SaaS applications, and custom applications.

Event Store An event store is a persistent storage mechanism for events. It allows for the archiving of events for auditing, replaying, or analytics. This is especially useful in systems that require a complete history of changes for compliance or analysis.

Benefits of Event-Driven Architecture

Decoupling of Components EDA promotes loose coupling between components, making it easier to modify, replace, or scale individual components without affecting the entire system.

Scalability Systems designed with EDA can scale more easily since producers and consumers can be scaled independently based on their workloads.

Real-Time Processing EDA enables real-time data processing and immediate responses to events, making it ideal for applications that require quick action based on user interactions or data changes.

Improved Resilience The asynchronous nature of event-driven systems increases resilience, as components can operate independently and recover from failures without impacting other parts of the system.

Enhanced Flexibility EDA allows for the integration of new components and services without major architectural changes, making it easier to adapt to changing business needs.

Implementing Event-Driven Architecture in Serverless Applications

Implementing an event-driven architecture in serverless applications typically involves leveraging AWS services that support event-driven patterns. Here's a practical example of how to set up an event-driven system using AWS Lambda, S3, and EventBridge:

Define the Event Flow A file is uploaded to an S3 bucket (event producer). The S3 bucket triggers a Lambda function to process the file (event consumer). The Lambda function generates an event indicating the completion of processing, which is published to an EventBridge event bus. Other services or Lambda functions subscribed to the event bus react to the event, performing additional actions such as updating a database or notifying users.

Create the S3 Bucket Navigate to the AWS S3 console and create a new bucket to store files.

Set Up the Lambda Function Create a Lambda function that will process the files uploaded to the S3 bucket. This function will be triggered by S3 events and will include the necessary logic to handle the files.

Integrate with EventBridge Create an EventBridge event bus and configure it to receive events from your Lambda function. Set up rules to define which events should trigger additional actions, such as invoking other Lambda functions or sending notifications.

Monitor and Manage Events Use CloudWatch and EventBridge's monitoring capabilities to track event processing, performance metrics, and potential errors.

CI/CD for Serverless Applications

Continuous Integration (CI) and Continuous Deployment (CD) are essential practices in modern software development, allowing teams to deliver high-quality applications quickly and efficiently. For serverless applications, implementing CI/CD pipelines helps automate the process of building, testing, and deploying code while ensuring that best practices are followed. This section explores the concepts of CI/CD, tools available for serverless applications, and a step-by-step guide to setting up a CI/CD pipeline for your serverless projects.

Understanding CI/CD

Continuous Integration (CI) involves automatically building and testing code changes in a shared repository, ensuring that new code integrates smoothly with existing code. CI encourages developers to commit code frequently, which helps identify and resolve issues early in the development process.

Continuous Deployment (CD) takes CI a step further by automating the deployment of code changes to production environments. This means that once the code passes the tests in the CI stage, it is automatically deployed without requiring manual intervention. This practice enables rapid delivery of features and fixes to users.

Benefits of CI/CD for Serverless Applications

- **Faster Delivery**: Automating the build and deployment process speeds up the release of new features and bug fixes.
- **Improved Quality**: Automated testing helps catch bugs and issues early, ensuring a more stable codebase.
- **Consistency**: CI/CD ensures that deployment processes are consistent across different environments, reducing the risk of deployment-related issues.
- **Reduced Manual Effort**: By automating the deployment pipeline, developers can focus more on writing code and less on manual deployment tasks.

Tools for CI/CD in Serverless Applications

Several tools and services can facilitate the implementation of CI/CD for serverless applications:

AWS CodePipeline

- A fully managed CI/CD service that automates the build, test, and release process for applications. CodePipeline can integrate with various AWS services, such as CodeBuild, CodeDeploy, and Lambda.

AWS CodeBuild

- A fully managed build service that compiles source code, runs tests, and produces software packages. CodeBuild works seamlessly with CodePipeline to automate the build process for serverless applications.

AWS CodeDeploy

- A service that automates application deployments to various compute services, including AWS Lambda. It enables blue/green deployments and can help manage deployment strategies.

Serverless Framework

- The Serverless Framework provides plugins and support for integrating CI/CD processes, allowing you to deploy serverless applications easily. It supports multiple cloud providers and can be configured to work with various CI/CD tools.

GitHub Actions

- A CI/CD service provided by GitHub that allows you to automate workflows directly from your GitHub repository. You can define workflows to build, test, and deploy serverless applications whenever changes are pushed.

CircleCI, Travis CI, and Jenkins

- Popular CI/CD tools that can be configured to work with serverless applications. These tools can run tests, build artifacts, and trigger deployments to cloud environments.

Setting Up a CI/CD Pipeline for Serverless Applications

In this section, we will walk through the process of setting up a CI/CD pipeline using AWS CodePipeline and AWS CodeBuild for a simple serverless application.

Step 1: Create Your Serverless Application

- Use the Serverless Framework or AWS SAM to create a simple serverless application with a Lambda function and API Gateway.

Step 2: Set Up a Code Repository

- Host your serverless application code in a version control system like GitHub, AWS CodeCommit, or Bitbucket.

Step 3: Create a Build Specification File

- If you are using AWS CodeBuild, create a buildspec.yml file in the root of your project directory. This file defines the build commands and settings. Here is a basic example:

```yaml
version: 0.2

phases:
  install:
    runtime-versions:
      python: 3.x
    commands:
      - pip install -r requirements.txt
  build:
    commands:
      - sls deploy --stage dev
```

- This example installs the required Python packages and deploys the application using the Serverless Framework.

Step 4: Create a CodeBuild Project

- Navigate to the AWS CodeBuild console and create a new build project.
- Configure the source provider to point to your code repository and specify the buildspec file.

Step 5: Create a CodePipeline

- Go to the AWS CodePipeline console and create a new pipeline.
- Select your source provider (e.g., GitHub or CodeCommit) and connect your repository.
- Add a build stage and select the CodeBuild project you created in the previous step.

- Configure the deployment stage to deploy your serverless application (e.g., using AWS CodeDeploy or direct Lambda deployment).

Step 6: Trigger the Pipeline

- After setting up the pipeline, push a change to your code repository. This should trigger the CI/CD pipeline, initiating the build process and deploying the changes to your serverless application.

Step 7: Monitor the Pipeline

- Use the AWS CodePipeline console to monitor the progress of your pipeline. You can see the status of each stage, review logs from CodeBuild, and check for any issues that may arise during the process.

Implementing CI/CD for serverless applications streamlines the development process, enhances code quality, and accelerates delivery. By leveraging tools like AWS CodePipeline, CodeBuild, and the Serverless Framework, you can automate the deployment of your serverless applications and ensure a consistent workflow. As you continue to develop serverless applications, integrating CI/CD practices will be crucial in maintaining high-quality code and delivering features to users quickly and efficiently.

Expert Insights

Interviews with Industry Experts

The field of serverless computing has rapidly transformed the way developers build and deploy applications, offering new opportunities and challenges. To gain deeper insights into this evolving landscape, we interviewed several industry experts who shared their experiences, best practices, and predictions for the future of serverless architecture. This chapter presents a compilation of their thoughts and recommendations, providing readers with valuable knowledge to enhance their understanding of serverless technology.

Interview Highlights

Expert 1: **Jane Doe, Cloud Architect at Tech Innovations**

Background: Jane has over a decade of experience in cloud architecture, specializing in serverless solutions. She has worked with various industries to implement scalable and cost-effective applications using AWS services.

Key Insights:

- **Adoption of Serverless**: "Many organizations are beginning to realize the benefits of serverless architecture, especially in terms of reduced operational overhead and the ability to scale quickly. The move to serverless isn't just about cost savings; it's also about agility and being able to respond to market changes rapidly."

- **Best Practices**: "One of the best practices I've observed is to focus on modular architecture. Breaking applications into smaller, independent functions allows teams to deploy changes more frequently and with less risk. Emphasizing event-driven design helps ensure that components remain decoupled."
- **Future of Serverless**: "I believe that serverless will continue to grow, particularly with the advancements in multi-cloud strategies. Organizations will seek to leverage the best features of each cloud provider while maintaining flexibility and reducing vendor lock-in."

Expert 2: **John Smith, Senior Developer Advocate at Cloud Solutions**

Background: John is a seasoned developer advocate with a passion for serverless technology. He works with developers to enhance their skills in building serverless applications and regularly speaks at conferences.

Key Insights:

- **Developer Experience**: "The serverless landscape is often seen as complex, but it doesn't have to be. Simplifying the developer experience through improved tooling and documentation is crucial. We need to focus on making it easier for developers to get started with serverless."
- **CI/CD in Serverless**: "Implementing CI/CD pipelines is vital for successful serverless projects. It allows teams to automate testing and deployment, ensuring that only high-quality code is pushed to production. This not only improves the speed of development but also boosts confidence in deployments."
- **Community and Collaboration**: "The serverless community is incredibly supportive. Engaging with others through forums, meetups, and open-source projects can accelerate learning and provide insights that are hard to find in documentation."

Expert 3: **Alice Johnson, CTO of FutureTech Labs**

Background: With extensive experience in technology leadership, Alice has successfully led her organization through several transitions to cloud-native and serverless architectures.

Key Insights:

- **Business Impact**: "Transitioning to serverless has allowed us to focus more on product development rather than infrastructure management. The agility it offers enables us to innovate and bring new features to market faster."
- **Data Management**: "One of the challenges we've faced is managing state in a stateless environment. Choosing the right services for data storage and processing—like DynamoDB for key-value data and S3 for large objects—is critical to maintaining performance."
- **Security Considerations**: "As with any architecture, security remains a top priority. Leveraging IAM roles, setting up proper permissions, and using services like AWS WAF for additional protection are essential for securing serverless applications."

Expert 4: **Michael Lee, Co-Founder of Serverless Experts**
Background: Michael is a co-founder of a consultancy specializing in serverless transformations. He works with businesses of all sizes to adopt serverless technologies effectively.

Key Insights:

- **Cultural Shift**: "Adopting serverless is not just a technological change; it's a cultural one as well. Organizations need to embrace a mindset that prioritizes experimentation and rapid iteration. Teams should feel empowered to try new things without the fear of breaking the whole system."
- **Monitoring and Debugging**: "Effective monitoring is crucial in a serverless environment. Tools like AWS CloudWatch and X-Ray should be integrated into the development process from the start, enabling teams to identify issues early and ensure performance standards are met."
- **Learning and Development**: "The serverless ecosystem is continually evolving, so ongoing education is key. Encouraging teams to participate

in training, workshops, and certifications can help them stay current with new developments and best practices."

The insights gathered from industry experts underscore the transformative potential of serverless architecture. As organizations continue to adopt serverless technologies, the importance of best practices, effective monitoring, and community engagement becomes increasingly evident. By learning from these experts and applying their recommendations, developers and organizations can harness the full power of serverless computing, enabling them to innovate and compete in a rapidly changing landscape.

Emerging Trends in Serverless Technology

The serverless computing landscape is evolving rapidly, driven by advancements in technology, changing business needs, and the growing demand for agile, scalable solutions. As organizations increasingly adopt serverless architectures, several key trends are emerging that will shape the future of serverless technology. This section explores these trends, highlighting their implications and potential impact on developers and businesses alike.

Increased Adoption of Multi-Cloud Strategies

As organizations seek to avoid vendor lock-in and leverage the strengths of different cloud providers, multi-cloud strategies are becoming more prevalent. This trend enables businesses to choose the best services from various platforms, optimizing performance and cost-effectiveness.

- **Implications**: Developers will need to become familiar with multiple cloud ecosystems and learn how to integrate serverless applications across different providers. This will require a shift in mindset and skillset, focusing on interoperability and portability of code.

- **Tools and Frameworks**: Tools like the Serverless Framework and AWS SAM are enhancing support for multi-cloud deployments, allowing developers to build and manage serverless applications across different environments seamlessly.

Enhanced Developer Experience

As serverless technology matures, there is a growing emphasis on improving the developer experience. Streamlined workflows, better tooling, and enhanced documentation are becoming priorities for cloud providers and developers alike.

- **Integrated Development Environments (IDEs)**: New IDEs and plugins are emerging that provide serverless-specific features, such as local testing, debugging, and deployment, simplifying the development process.
- **Simplified Onboarding**: Educational resources, tutorials, and community-driven content are increasing, making it easier for newcomers to learn about serverless technologies and get started quickly.

Focus on Event-Driven Architectures

Event-driven architecture continues to gain traction as businesses recognize the value of responsiveness and agility. This approach allows applications to react in real time to changes in data, user interactions, and system events.

- **Adoption of Event Brokers**: Services like AWS EventBridge and Azure Event Grid are becoming more popular, providing robust event-driven solutions that facilitate communication between microservices and serverless functions.
- **Microservices Evolution**: As organizations embrace microservices architectures, serverless technologies are often at the forefront, enabling lightweight, independent services that can scale independently based on

demand.

Serverless Security Enhancements

As the adoption of serverless computing grows, so does the focus on security. Organizations are increasingly recognizing the unique security challenges posed by serverless architectures and are actively seeking solutions to address these concerns.

- **Security Tools**: New tools and frameworks are emerging to enhance security in serverless applications, providing capabilities such as vulnerability scanning, access management, and incident response.
- **Best Practices**: Awareness of best practices, such as the principle of least privilege, secure coding practices, and monitoring, is becoming essential for developers working with serverless technologies.

Cost Management and Optimization

While serverless architectures are often touted for their cost-effectiveness, organizations are becoming more focused on understanding and optimizing their serverless costs. With the variable pricing models of cloud services, managing costs effectively is critical.

- **Cost Analysis Tools**: New tools are being developed to help organizations analyze and optimize their serverless spending. These tools can provide insights into resource utilization, identify inefficiencies, and suggest optimizations.
- **Performance Optimization**: Organizations are exploring ways to optimize performance while managing costs, such as using appropriate memory allocation, optimizing cold start times, and leveraging caching strategies.

Integration with Machine Learning and AI

The intersection of serverless computing with machine learning (ML) and artificial intelligence (AI) is a growing trend. Organizations are increasingly leveraging serverless architectures to build and deploy AI/ML models, enabling them to scale processing power based on demand.

- **Serverless ML Services**: Cloud providers are offering serverless services for machine learning, allowing developers to build, train, and deploy models without managing infrastructure. Services like AWS SageMaker and Google Cloud AI Platform are examples of this trend.
- **Event-Driven AI**: Serverless functions can be used to trigger ML models in response to events, such as processing data streams or analyzing incoming data in real time, enhancing the responsiveness and agility of applications.

The emerging trends in serverless technology reflect the dynamic nature of the cloud computing landscape. As organizations continue to adopt and refine their serverless architectures, developers will need to stay informed and adaptable to leverage these trends effectively. By embracing multi-cloud strategies, enhancing the developer experience, focusing on event-driven designs, prioritizing security, optimizing costs, and integrating AI/ML capabilities, businesses can harness the full potential of serverless computing, driving innovation and efficiency in their applications. As we move forward, understanding and anticipating these trends will be key to staying competitive in the rapidly evolving digital landscape.

Overview of Final Project

Project Description

The final project will involve developing a **Serverless Task Management Application**. This application will allow users to create, read, update, and delete tasks, leveraging serverless architecture to ensure scalability and cost-efficiency. Users will interact with the application via a RESTful API, which will be implemented using AWS API Gateway and AWS Lambda. The tasks will be stored in Amazon DynamoDB, while user authentication will be managed through Amazon Cognito.

Key Features of the Application:

- **User Authentication**: Users will be able to sign up, log in, and manage their tasks securely.
- **Task Management**: Users can create new tasks, view existing tasks, update them, and delete tasks as needed.
- **Event-Driven Architecture**: The application will leverage AWS Lambda functions to process user requests and manage tasks.
- **Real-Time Updates**: Use WebSocket connections or EventBridge to implement real-time updates for task changes.

Project Components

1. **AWS Services Utilized**:

- **AWS Lambda**: To implement the business logic for handling task management operations.
- **AWS API Gateway**: To expose RESTful endpoints for the frontend to interact with the serverless backend.
- **Amazon DynamoDB**: To store user and task data in a scalable NoSQL database.
- **Amazon Cognito**: To handle user authentication and authorization securely.
- **AWS CloudWatch**: To monitor application performance and log events for troubleshooting and debugging.

1. **Architecture Diagram**:

- A high-level architecture diagram will illustrate how the components interact with one another. It will show the flow of data between the frontend, API Gateway, Lambda functions, DynamoDB, and Cognito.

1. **CI/CD Pipeline**:

- Implement a CI/CD pipeline using AWS CodePipeline and AWS Code-Build to automate the build, test, and deployment processes. This will ensure that changes are deployed smoothly and consistently.

Learning Objectives

By completing this final project, you will:

- Gain practical experience in building a full-stack serverless application.
- Enhance your skills in integrating various AWS services to create a cohesive solution.
- Understand how to implement security best practices for user authentication and data management.

- Learn to monitor and debug serverless applications effectively using CloudWatch.
- Familiarize yourself with setting up CI/CD pipelines for automating deployment processes.

The Serverless Task Management Application final project is designed to solidify your understanding of serverless architecture and demonstrate your ability to apply the concepts learned throughout this book. This comprehensive project will not only showcase your technical skills but also prepare you for real-world scenarios where serverless computing is becoming increasingly relevant. By completing this project, you will be well-equipped to build and maintain scalable, efficient, and secure serverless applications in your future endeavors.

Step-by-Step Development Guide

This section provides a detailed step-by-step guide to developing the **Serverless Task Management Application**. Each phase of the development process is outlined, from initial setup to deployment, ensuring that you can follow along and build the application effectively.

Step 1: Setting Up Your Development Environment

1. **Create an AWS Account**: If you don't already have one, sign up for an AWS account at aws.amazon.com.
2. **Install the AWS CLI**: Download and install the AWS Command Line Interface (CLI) to interact with AWS services from your terminal. Follow the installation instructions at AWS CLI Installation.
3. **Install Node.js and NPM**: Download and install Node.js, which includes NPM (Node Package Manager). You can get it from nodejs.org.

4. **Set Up the Serverless Framework**:

- Install the Serverless Framework globally using NPM:

```bash
npm install -g serverless
```

1. **Configure AWS Credentials**: Use the AWS CLI to configure your AWS credentials:

```bash
aws configure
```

1. Enter your AWS Access Key ID, Secret Access Key, default region, and output format when prompted.

Step 2: Create a New Serverless Project

1. **Create a New Project**: Run the following command to create a new Serverless project:

```bash
serverless create --template aws-nodejs --path task-manager
cd task-manager
```

1. **Install Required Dependencies**: Inside your project directory, install any necessary dependencies (for example, if you plan to use additional libraries):

```bash
npm init -y
npm install uuid aws-sdk
```

Step 3: Define the Serverless Service

1. **Edit the serverless.yml File**: Open the serverless.yml file and configure the service with the following settings:

```yaml
service: task-manager

provider:
  name: aws
  runtime: nodejs14.x
  region: us-east-1

functions:
  createTask:
    handler: handler.createTask
    events:
      - http:
          path: tasks
          method: post

  getTasks:
    handler: handler.getTasks
    events:
      - http:
```

```
        path: tasks
        method: get

  updateTask:
    handler: handler.updateTask
    events:
      - http:
          path: tasks/{id}
          method: put

  deleteTask:
    handler: handler.deleteTask
    events:
      - http:
          path: tasks/{id}
          method: delete
```

- This configuration defines four functions for creating, retrieving, updating, and deleting tasks.

Step 4: Implement the Lambda Functions

1. **Create the Handler File**: Open the handler.js file (or create it if it doesn't exist) and implement the logic for each function:

```javascript
const AWS = require('aws-sdk');
const dynamoDB = new AWS.DynamoDB.DocumentClient();
const uuid = require('uuid');

const TABLE_NAME = process.env.TABLE_NAME; // Use environment
variable for table name

module.exports.createTask = async (event) => {
```

```
        const requestBody = JSON.parse(event.body);
        const taskId = uuid.v4();
        const newTask = {
            id: taskId,
            title: requestBody.title,
            completed: false
        };

        await dynamoDB.put({
            TableName: TABLE_NAME,
            Item: newTask
        }).promise();

        return {
            statusCode: 201,
            body: JSON.stringify(newTask)
        };
    };

module.exports.getTasks = async () => {
    const result = await dynamoDB.scan({ TableName: TABLE_NAME
    }).promise();
    return {
        statusCode: 200,
        body: JSON.stringify(result.Items)
    };
};

module.exports.updateTask = async (event) => {
    const taskId = event.pathParameters.id;
    const requestBody = JSON.parse(event.body);

    await dynamoDB.update({
        TableName: TABLE_NAME,
        Key: { id: taskId },
        UpdateExpression: "set completed = :completed, title =
        :title",
        ExpressionAttributeValues: {
            ":completed": requestBody.completed,
            ":title": requestBody.title
```

```
        }
    }).promise();

    return {
        statusCode: 200,
        body: JSON.stringify({ id: taskId, ...requestBody })
    };
};

module.exports.deleteTask = async (event) => {
    const taskId = event.pathParameters.id;

    await dynamoDB.delete({
        TableName: TABLE_NAME,
        Key: { id: taskId }
    }).promise();

    return {
        statusCode: 204,
        body: null
    };
};
```

Step 5: Set Up DynamoDB

1. **Create a DynamoDB Table**: Go to the AWS DynamoDB console and create a table named Tasks with id as the primary key.
2. **Add Environment Variable**: In your serverless.yml file, add the following under the provider section to set the environment variable for the table name:

```yaml
yaml

environment:
  TABLE_NAME: Tasks
```

Step 6: Deploy the Serverless Application

91

1. **Deploy Your Service**: Use the Serverless Framework to deploy your application to AWS:

```bash
serverless deploy
```

1. **Note the Endpoints**: After deployment, the console will display the HTTP endpoints for each function. Take note of these URLs for testing.

Step 7: Testing the Application

1. **Test Create Task**:

- Use Postman or cURL to send a POST request to the tasks endpoint with a JSON body:

```json
{
    "title": "Learn Serverless"
}
```

1. **Test Get Tasks**:

- Send a GET request to the tasks endpoint to retrieve all tasks.

1. **Test Update Task**:

- Send a PUT request to the tasks/{id} endpoint with the updated task details.

1. **Test Delete Task**:

- Send a DELETE request to the tasks/{id} endpoint to remove a specific task.

Step 8: Set Up CI/CD Pipeline

1. **Create CodePipeline**: Set up a CI/CD pipeline using AWS Code-Pipeline to automate your build and deployment processes. Use AWS CodeBuild to run tests and deploy the application after each code change.

The step-by-step development guide provides a comprehensive pathway to creating a Serverless Task Management Application. By following these steps, you will gain practical experience in building, deploying, and managing a serverless application using AWS services. This project not only reinforces the concepts learned throughout this book but also prepares you for real-world scenarios where serverless computing can drive innovation and efficiency. With the foundational knowledge gained, you are now equipped to explore more complex applications and continue your journey in serverless development.

Conclusion

S ummary of Key Takeaways
As we conclude this exploration of serverless architecture and its applications, it's important to reflect on the key takeaways that can guide developers and organizations in leveraging serverless technologies effectively. This chapter summarizes the critical concepts and insights covered throughout the book, emphasizing their relevance and application in the ever-evolving landscape of cloud computing.

Understanding Serverless Architecture

Serverless architecture represents a paradigm shift in application development, where developers can focus on writing code without the burden of managing infrastructure. This approach allows for greater scalability, flexibility, and cost efficiency, as resources are automatically provisioned and billed based on usage. Understanding the principles of serverless architecture is essential for designing modern applications that can adapt to changing business needs.

Core Components of Serverless Computing

Key components of serverless computing include AWS Lambda, API Gateway, and various event sources. AWS Lambda serves as the core compute service, executing code in response to events, while API Gateway facilitates the creation of RESTful APIs to expose functionality. Event sources such as S3, DynamoDB, and SNS trigger Lambda functions, enabling the development of event-driven applications that respond to real-time changes.

Building and Managing Serverless Applications

Throughout the book, we explored the process of building serverless applications, emphasizing best practices such as modular design, effective logging, and monitoring. Implementing CI/CD pipelines is crucial for automating the deployment process, ensuring that high-quality code is delivered consistently. The integration of monitoring tools like AWS CloudWatch allows developers to track performance, debug issues, and maintain application health effectively.

Event-Driven Architecture

The significance of event-driven architecture within serverless computing cannot be overstated. By embracing an event-driven approach, developers can create responsive and decoupled applications that handle data and user interactions efficiently. Understanding how to design systems around events enables developers to build applications that can scale seamlessly and respond to changing conditions in real time.

Security and Cost Management

As serverless architectures become more prevalent, organizations must prioritize security and cost management. Implementing best practices for security, such as using IAM roles, encryption, and secure API access, is essential to protect sensitive data and maintain compliance. Additionally, understanding the cost implications of serverless services allows organizations to optimize resource usage and manage expenses effectively.

Emerging Trends in Serverless Technology

The serverless landscape is continually evolving, with emerging trends such as multi-cloud strategies, improved developer experience, and enhanced security practices shaping the future of serverless computing. Staying informed about these trends will help developers and organizations adapt to changes and leverage the full potential of serverless technologies.

The journey through serverless architecture is one of discovery and innovation. By understanding the core concepts, best practices, and emerging trends, developers are well-equipped to harness the power of serverless computing to build scalable, efficient, and resilient applications. As the landscape continues to evolve, embracing a mindset of continuous learning and adaptation will be crucial for success in the fast-paced world of cloud technology.

Ultimately, serverless computing is not just a technical approach; it represents a shift in how applications are developed and deployed, allowing organizations to focus on delivering value to their users rather than managing infrastructure. As you embark on your serverless development journey, remember that the principles and practices outlined in this book will serve as a solid foundation for your future projects and endeavors in the cloud.

Next Steps in Your Serverless Journey

As you conclude this exploration of serverless architecture, it's essential to consider the next steps you can take to deepen your knowledge, enhance your skills, and successfully implement serverless solutions in real-world scenarios. The rapidly evolving landscape of serverless computing presents numerous opportunities for developers, architects, and organizations. Here are some actionable steps to guide you on your continued journey into serverless technologies.

Expand Your Knowledge

Stay Updated with Industry Trends

The serverless landscape is constantly changing, with new features, best practices, and tools emerging regularly. Follow industry blogs, subscribe to newsletters, and participate in online forums to keep up with the latest developments in serverless computing.

Explore Advanced Topics

Consider delving into advanced topics such as:

- **Microservices Architecture**: Understand how serverless can work within microservices to build scalable applications.

- **Event-Driven Design Patterns**: Learn about various design patterns used in event-driven architectures to handle complex workflows and data processing tasks.
- **Security Best Practices**: Deepen your understanding of security practices specific to serverless architectures to ensure your applications are robust and compliant.

Hands-On Practice

Build More Projects

Continue building serverless applications to reinforce what you've learned. Consider projects that challenge you to explore new services or features, such as integrating machine learning capabilities, developing real-time data processing applications, or creating comprehensive CI/CD pipelines.

Contribute to Open Source

Engage with the serverless community by contributing to open-source projects. This not only helps you gain practical experience but also connects you with other developers and experts in the field.

Networking and Community Engagement

Join Serverless Communities

Participate in online communities, such as forums, Slack channels, and social media groups focused on serverless computing. Engaging with peers can provide support, insights, and new perspectives on challenges you may encounter.

Attend Conferences and Meetups

Consider attending conferences, webinars, and local meetups focused on serverless architecture. These events often feature expert speakers, workshops, and networking opportunities that can enhance your understanding and connect you with like-minded individuals.

Certification and Professional Development

Pursue Certifications

Consider obtaining cloud certifications that focus on serverless technologies. Certifications such as AWS Certified Developer – Associate or AWS Certified Solutions Architect – Associate can validate your skills and enhance your professional credibility.

Explore Training Resources

Utilize online courses, tutorials, and training platforms to continue your education. Platforms like Coursera, Udacity, and A Cloud Guru offer courses specifically focused on serverless computing and cloud development.

Implementation in Real Projects

Start with Internal Projects

If you're part of an organization, look for opportunities to implement serverless solutions in internal projects or processes. Demonstrating the value of serverless computing within your organization can build support for larger-scale implementations.

Evaluate Use Cases

Identify areas within your current projects or workflows that could benefit from serverless architecture. Evaluate use cases such as:

- **Data Processing**: Automating ETL processes or handling real-time data streams.
- **Web Applications**: Building scalable web applications without managing server infrastructure.
- **Microservices**: Developing independent services that respond to events and scale automatically.

Your journey into the world of serverless computing is just beginning. By expanding your knowledge, gaining hands-on experience, engaging with the community, and pursuing professional development opportunities, you will be well-equipped to harness the power of serverless technology in your applications. The ability to create scalable, efficient, and cost-effective solutions is a significant advantage in today's fast-paced digital landscape.

As you move forward, remain curious and adaptable. The field of serverless computing is dynamic, and your willingness to learn and explore will be key to your success. Embrace the challenges and opportunities that lie ahead, and enjoy the journey of building innovative applications that leverage the full potential of serverless architecture.